CONTEXT CLUES & FIGURATIVE LANGUAGE

by Linda Ward Beech

NEW YORK • TORONTO • LONDON • AUCKLAND • SYDNEY
MEXICO CITY • NEW DELHI • HONG KONG • BUENOS AIRES

Teaching *Resources*

Cover design by Maria Lilja
Interior design by Sydney Wright
Interior illustrations by Mike Gordon

ISBN-13 978-0-439-55410-7
ISBN-10 0-439-55410-1

11 12 13 14 15 16 17 18 19 20   40   14 13 12 11 10

Contents

Introduction

Reading comprehension involves numerous thinking skills. Among these skills are a reader's use of context clues and his or her facility at deriving meaning from figurative language. The reader who is adept at using context clues to understand word meaning is in a position to make sense of a text and read with ease and efficiency. The reader who can differentiate between literal and figurative language and then determine the meaning of figures of speech, may well be on the way to fluency. In this book, Exercises 1–18 help students learn to recognize context clues in order to decipher word meaning and to build vocabulary. Exercises 19–35 focus on practice with figurative language. Use pages 8 and 9 after you introduce the skills to give students help in understanding them.

Using This Book

Pages 8–9

After introducing context clues and figurative language to students (see pages 6 and 7), duplicate and pass out pages 8 and 9. Use page 8 to help students review what they have learned about using context clues. By explaining their thinking, students are using metacognition to analyze how they recognized and utilized these clues. Page 9 helps students review what they have learned about figurative language.

Pages 10–27

These pages provide practice in using **context clues**. Students read a paragraph. The first question asks them to identify the missing word from the paragraph. The second question requires students to figure out the meaning of a particular word (in boldface) from the paragraph. In the third and fourth questions, students underline the language that helped them determine the boldfaced word's intended meaning and then show their understanding by writing a sentence of their own using that word.

Pages 28–44

These pages provide practice in recognizing and comprehending **figurative language**. To get started, students read a paragraph. The first question asks students to identify the type of figurative language the underlined figure of speech represents. The second question provides students with practice pinpointing what images the author is describing or comparing. The third, fourth, and fifth questions invite students to identify another example of figurative language in the same paragraph and then to explain the meaning of the figure of speech.

Pages 45–46

Once students complete the practice pages, use these pages to assess their progress.

Page 47

You may wish to keep a record of students' progress. Sample comments that will help you guide students to improving skills might include:

- reads carelessly
- misunderstands text
- has difficulty recognizing context clues
- does not apply prior knowledge
- overlooks figures of speech
- needs help with visualizing

> **Teacher Tip**
>
> For students who need extra help, you might suggest that they keep pages 8 and 9 with them to refer to when they complete the exercises.

> **Teacher Tip**
>
> Students can learn a lot if you review the finished exercises with them on a regular basis. Encourage students to explain their thinking for each correct answer. Ask them to share the context clues that helped them decide what the meaning of a word is. Engage students in discussing how they came up with their sentences using the word.

Teaching About Context Clues

1. Introduce the concept: Write this sentence on the board.

> **Although Megan was late for class, she did not have a good _____ for her tardiness.**

Invite students to supply a word for the blank in the sentence.

2. Model thinking: After students have suggested words such as *reason, excuse,* or *alibi* for the sentence, continue the lesson by thinking aloud.

> You're not supposed to be late for a class. If you're late, you should have a good reason or excuse.

> These words make sense in the sentence.

3. Define the skill: Remind students that in determining an appropriate word to use in the blank, they examined the other words in the sentence for clues. Point out that the word *although* is a clue that Megan shouldn't have been late for class unless she had a good reason. *Tardiness* is something you need to explain to those kept waiting.

Explain that when readers take into account context, they are thinking about the ideas presented in the text. When students read a passage and come to an unfamiliar word, they can use context clues to try to figure out the word's meaning. These context clues can be in the same sentence or in other sentences in the passage. Share these examples of context clues with students:

- The meaning is clearly given.
  *Growers try to ship fruit that is **perishable** quickly.*
  Perishable fruit is produce that spoils or rots easily.

- An example is given.
  *The government needs to increase its **revenues**. For example, it hopes to get more income from taxpayers.*

- The meaning is restated.
  *Marco found it hard to **gauge**, or <u>determine</u>, the speed of the ball.*

- Other words help describe a word.
  *The **fragile** teacup shattered because it was <u>delicate</u> and <u>frail</u>.*

- The word has a known prefix or suffix.
  *Lila did exercises to keep her muscles **flexible**.*

- The word is contrasted with a word of opposite meaning.
  *When the captain shouted an order, many **idle** people became <u>busy</u>.*

6

Teaching About Figurative Language

1. Introduce the concept: Write these sentences on the board.

> **The snow on the lawn was like frosting on a cake.**
>
> **The snow on the lawn was a thick, white frosting.**
>
> **The snow tucked a white blanket over the lawn.**
>
> **The snow on the lawn was piled in mountain-high drifts.**

Ask students to explain what the sentences are about.

2. Model thinking: Think aloud as you guide students in recognizing that each of these sentences, while describing snow on a lawn, helps the reader shape an individual mental image.

> The first two sentences help me see the snow as white frosting. The third sentence creates the sense of the snow placing a white blanket on the lawn, and the last sentence makes me see lots of snow in high drifts.

3. Define the skill: Tell students that writers sometimes use figurative language to give power to their words and to create compelling, dramatic descriptions. Examples of figurative language covered in this book are similes, metaphors, personification, and hyperbole.

- A **simile** is a statement comparing things using the words *like* or *as*. The first sentence is a simile. A simile tells what something is like. *The <u>snow</u> was like <u>frosting</u>.*

- A **metaphor** is also a statement comparing things. A metaphor says that one thing is another thing; it does not use *like* or *as*. The second sentence is a metaphor. *The <u>snow</u> was <u>frosting</u>.*

- **Personification** is a statement that attributes a human trait or action to a nonliving thing. The third sentence includes an example of personification. *The <u>snow</u> <u>tucked</u> a white blanket over the lawn.*

- **Hyperbole** is a statement of exaggeration. The last sentence is an example of hyperbole. *The <u>snow</u> was piled in <u>mountain-high</u> drifts.*

Name _____   Date _____

What Are Context Clues?

When you read a paragraph, you often come to words that you don't know. How does a reader figure out word meaning? One way is by looking for context clues. A reader might think:

What is this sentence or paragraph about? How is this word used in the sentence or paragraph? What part of speech is the word? What is its relationship to the topic?

What other words in the sentence and paragraph suggest possible meanings? What clues can I find? What word(s) can I substitute that makes sense?

These questions help a reader use **context**. Context is the setting in which a word appears. The context for a word can be a sentence or a paragraph. It can also be a longer passage.

Read the paragraphs.

Castles in the Middle Ages had one main _____. They were built for protection. The many people living within a castle worried about war at all times.

1 The best word for the blank is

   (A) communal   (B) purpose   (C) delight   (D) medieval

   • Which words are the wrong part of speech? _____

   • Which word doesn't make sense? _____

A castle was surrounded by outer walls and inner walls. Tall, round towers stood at the corners of the outer walls. The inner walls enclosed the **bailey**. Much of the castle life took place in this outdoor area within the walls.

2 In this paragraph, the word **bailey** must mean

   (A) drawbridge   (B) family   (C) apprentice   (D) courtyard

3 Underline the words in the paragraph that helped you with the meaning of **bailey**.

Scholastic Teaching Resources   Context Clues & Figurative Language

What Is Figurative Language?

Sometimes writers use figurative language to create vivid descriptions. Figurative language is the use of words in ways apart from their ordinary meanings. The words or phrases do not mean exactly, or literally, what they say. Instead, they create impressions by suggesting comparisons, unlikely actions, or exaggerations that make the reader take notice.

Use these tips to understand figurative language:

1. Identify the type of figurative language being used.

Simile	Mackenzie was as tired-looking as wilted lettuce.
Metaphor	Wilbur was a library of information.
Personification	The tree roots slurped up the heavy rain.
Hyperbole	Our cat Jinx ruled the entire household.

2. Determine the literal meaning of the figure of speech.

Simile	Mackenzie was really weary.
Metaphor	Wilbur knew a lot.
Personification	The trees needed rain.
Hyperbole	Jinx got his own way.

Read the paragraph.

You could see the traffic for miles ahead. Every few minutes the cars would move a couple of feet, then come to a halt. "This is awful!" wept Andrea. "We'll never get home. <u>The cars are lined up all the way to the West Coast!</u>"

1 Identify the type of figurative language represented in the underlined words.

   Ⓐ simile   Ⓑ metaphor   Ⓒ personification   Ⓓ hyperbole

2 Explain what the figure of speech means. _____

_____

Context Clues

Read the paragraph. Answer the questions.

Leopards hunt for their food at night. These animals are carnivores and eat only meat. Their excellent eyesight helps them _____ and capture their prey even in the dark. In many cases, a leopard will carry its prey long distances away from the place of the kill. Because it is a good climber, a leopard will often drag its dinner into a tree where other animals cannot reach it. There, the leopard can devour its meal alone. Unlike lions, leopards are solitary and **antisocial** animals.

1 The best word for the blank in this paragraph is

Ⓐ hunger   Ⓑ purchase   Ⓒ stalk   Ⓓ discard

2 In this paragraph, the word **antisocial** must mean

Ⓐ friendly and likable   Ⓒ extremely hungry

Ⓑ enjoying groups   Ⓓ not sociable

3 Underline a word or words that helped you answer item 2.

4 Write a sentence of your own using the word **antisocial**.

_____

_____

_____

Context Clues

Read the paragraph. Answer the questions.

The earliest museums were really cabinets of "curiosities." They contained various things assembled by people of wealth. The first of these museums opened to the public in 1683 in Oxford, England. It was called the Ashmolean Museum. Its _____ included such curiosities as a stuffed dodo bird and a set of medieval armor. Visitors paid a fee upon leaving the museum. This fee was determined by the **duration** of the visitor's stay in the museum admiring the exhibits.

1 The best word for the blank in this paragraph is

Ⓐ collection   Ⓑ tourist   Ⓒ unique   Ⓓ ticket

2 In this paragraph, the word **duration** must mean

Ⓐ other guests   Ⓒ length of time

Ⓑ amount of fun   Ⓓ kind of place

3 Underline a word or words that helped you answer item 2.

4 Write a sentence of your own using the word **duration**.

_____

_____

_____

Context Clues

Read the paragraph. Answer the questions.

For hundreds of years, the Uro Indians of Peru have used the totora plant for many things. This plant, a kind of reed, grows in water. The Uro _____ on it as a source of food, building material, medicine, and fuel. The Indians use the totora to form islands in a lake. They then build their homes from the totora plant on the islands. These floating homelands require a lot of upkeep, though. As the totora plants rot in the water, the Uro must constantly **replenish** them with fresh reeds.

1 The best word for the blank in this paragraph is

Ⓐ cultivate   Ⓑ cultural   Ⓒ dominate   Ⓓ depend

2 In this paragraph, the word **replenish** must mean

Ⓐ fertilize   Ⓒ go through

Ⓑ replace   Ⓓ resemble

3 Underline a word or words that helped you answer item 2.

4 Write a sentence of your own using the word **replenish**.

_____

_____

_____

Scholastic Teaching Resources   Context Clues & Figurative Language

Name _____   Date _____

Context Clues

Read the paragraph. Answer the questions.

The sloth lives in the trees of tropical forests in Central America. It spends much of its time hanging upside down from branches. A sloth moves very slowly, feeding on leaves and fruit as it goes. During the rainy season, a sloth has a greenish _____. Tiny plants called green algae live in the sloth's fur where they capture moisture from the rain. The algae provide **camouflage** for the sloth in the green treetops. Being able to blend in is very helpful because a sloth could never move quickly enough to escape its enemies.

1 The best word for the blank in this paragraph is

Ⓐ experience   Ⓑ tinge   Ⓒ offspring   Ⓓ nutrition

2 In this paragraph, the word **camouflage** must mean

Ⓐ concealment   Ⓒ transportation

Ⓑ flesh-eating   Ⓓ entertainment

3 Underline a word or words that helped you answer item 2.

4 Write a sentence of your own using the word **camouflage**.

_____

_____

_____

EXERCISE

5

Context Clues

Read the paragraph. Answer the questions.

Watch out for cyclones! These violent
tropical storms can cause enormous
_____. Other names for cyclones
are *hurricanes* and *typhoons*. They
usually begin in areas of low pressure near the equator where the sea is especially
warm. Warm air rushes toward these areas and swirls upward in circles over
the sea. Within the center of this spinning mass is the eye of the storm. Around
the eye rage fierce winds and **torrential** rains. When cyclones hit land, they can
flatten buildings, rip off roofs, and wash away roads.

1 The best word for the blank in this paragraph is

Ⓐ wonder   Ⓑ moisture   Ⓒ destruction   Ⓓ deafening

2 In this paragraph, the word **torrential** must mean

Ⓐ soft and gentle   Ⓒ slow and steady

Ⓑ very heavy   Ⓓ really warm

3 Underline a word or words that helped you answer item 2.

4 Write a sentence of your own using the word **torrential**.

_____

_____

_____

Scholastic Teaching Resources   *Context Clues & Figurative Language*

Context Clues

Read the paragraph. Answer the questions.

At holiday time, many people hang mistletoe. With its dark green leaves and red berries, this plant is very _____. But what many people don't know is that mistletoe is a **parasite**. Instead of making its own food, it steals from other plants. The seeds of a mistletoe stick to the branches of trees. In time, they send roots into the tree's bark. The roots suck up nutrients for a new mistletoe. Often, several mistletoe plants will grow and live off the same tree. Sometimes this results in the death of the tree.

1 The best word for the blank in this paragraph is

Ⓐ formal   Ⓑ imperial   Ⓒ affectionate   Ⓓ festive

2 In this paragraph, the word **parasite** must mean

Ⓐ an organism that lives off others   Ⓒ a plant that supports others

Ⓑ a pretty sun umbrella   Ⓓ a popular holiday plant

3 Underline a word or words that helped you answer item 2.

4 Write a sentence of your own using the word **parasite**.

_____

_____

_____

EXERCISE

7

Context Clues

Read the paragraph. Answer the questions.

President Franklin D. Roosevelt (1883–1945) loved trees. As a boy, he took great interest in his family's land in Hyde Park, New York. He learned the importance of _____ the land. Later, as president, he created job programs for unemployed people in the field of conservation. During the early 1930s, **catastrophic** dust storms had stripped away valuable soil in the Great Plains. Roosevelt's programs taught farmers how to protect the soil and how to plant trees as windbreaks to keep the soil from blowing away.

1 The best word for the blank in this paragraph is

(A) destroying   (B) preserving   (C) encouraging   (D) delicate

2 In this paragraph, the word **catastrophic** must mean

(A) drought-resistant   (C) rather mild

(B) really disastrous   (D) greatly welcomed

3 Underline a word or words that helped you answer item 2.

4 Write a sentence of your own using the word **catastrophic**.

_____

_____

_____

Scholastic Teaching Resources   Context Clues & Figurative Language

Context Clues

Read the paragraph. Answer the questions.

People have been voting for their leaders since at least 500 B.C. Some of the earliest voters were ancient Greek citizens. They voted by dropping clay balls into pots for the _____ of their choice. Centuries later, Roman citizens voted with beans. Early settlers in North America used corn kernels. In the 1800s, people marked their choices on paper **ballots**. By 1892, voters were using machines with levers, and in the 1960s punch cards became common. Today, electronic voting is becoming widespread.

1 The best word for the blank in this paragraph is

(A) candidates   (B) elections   (C) stew   (D) authentic

2 In this paragraph, the word **ballot** must mean

(A) a song sung by wandering groups   (C) a printed page for registering a vote

(B) a kind of dance on toe shoes   (D) a pen used by people voting

3 Underline a word or words that helped you answer item 2.

4 Write a sentence of your own using the word **ballot**.

_____

_____

_____

Name _____   Date _____

Context Clues

Read the paragraph. Answer the questions.

No doubt you have read about exciting new buildings designed by famous _____. But did you know that most buildings are made for everyday use by ordinary people? Many types of homes are built in a **vernacular** style. This means their design is traditional to the group that builds them. For example, the Pueblo in the Southwest used adobe homes to shield people from the sun. Many pioneers cut the prairie soil into blocks to build sod houses on the treeless plains. In wooded areas, settlers put up log houses similar to those they had used back in Europe.

1 The best word for the blank in this paragraph is

Ⓐ actors   Ⓑ sculptors   Ⓒ architects   Ⓓ blueprints

2 In this paragraph, the word **vernacular** must mean

Ⓐ particular design   Ⓒ contemporary model

Ⓑ spectacular plan   Ⓓ native to a culture

3 Underline a word or words that helped you answer item 2.

4 Write a sentence of your own using the word **vernacular**.

_____

_____

_____

Context Clues

Read the paragraph. Answer the questions.

Want to hear some wild music? Listen to the CD of the Thai Elephant Orchestra. Elephants are known for their keen hearing and ability to make a wide range of sounds. The six animals in this group play sturdy versions of Thai instruments. For their CD, they had five practice _____ and then began recording. The conductor told the elephants when to stop and start but let them play as they wished. The "musicians" **improvised** as they played. Proceeds from the sale of the CD go into a bank for orphan elephants.

1 The best word for the blank in this paragraph is

Ⓐ instruments   Ⓑ composers   Ⓒ sessions   Ⓓ schedules

2 In this paragraph, the word **improvised** must mean

Ⓐ improved steadily   Ⓒ followed a musical score

Ⓑ invented without preparation   Ⓓ apologized for mistakes

3 Underline a word or words that helped you answer item 2.

4 Write a sentence of your own using the word **improvise**.

_____

_____

_____

Name _____   Date _____

Context Clues

Read the paragraph. Answer the questions.

Most people like a good hug now and then, but Jayson
Littman thinks some people are hug-deprived. To make
sure people get enough hugs, Jayson goes to a park in
New York City on Sundays. There, he _____ free hugs
to passersby. Some people like the idea, while others walk
right by him. However, Jayson doesn't mind. He smiles
broadly and holds out his arms to **entice** people. "Come
on! Everyone needs a hug," he says. Jayson's goal is to
start a national hugging movement.

1 The best word for the blank in this paragraph is

  Ⓐ withholds   Ⓑ embraces   Ⓒ quirky   Ⓓ offers

2 In this paragraph, the word **entice** must mean

  Ⓐ attract or lure   Ⓒ discourage

  Ⓑ entertain   Ⓓ frighten

3 Underline a word or words that helped you answer item 2.

4 Write a sentence of your own using the word **entice**.

_____

_____

_____

Scholastic Teaching Resources   *Context Clues & Figurative Language*

Context Clues

Read the paragraph. Answer the questions.

Have you ever played marbles? Some people take the game very seriously. Each year, students in Ohio _____ in the Akron District Marble Tournament. This is the oldest children's sporting event in the United States. Winners go on to a national event held annually in New Jersey. Today, most players use glass marbles, but in the past other materials have been **in vogue**. Popular materials for early marbles were clay, precious stones, and even a form of china.

1 The best word for the blank in this paragraph is

Ⓐ competition   Ⓑ compete   Ⓒ celebrate   Ⓓ community

2 In this paragraph, the words **in vogue** must mean

Ⓐ a variety of things   Ⓒ mass-produced

Ⓑ a kind of tournament   Ⓓ in style or fashion

3 Underline a word or words that helped you answer item 2.

4 Write a sentence of your own using the words **in vogue**.

_____

_____

_____

Context Clues

Read the paragraph. Answer the questions.

Many things make scientists curious.
For example, from time to time, large
white blobs wash up onto beaches around
the world. What are they? The _____ of
a huge octopus? A giant squid? A sea
monster? No one has ever been sure. Then, in 2003 a jelly-like blob washed up
on the coast of Chile. This time a team of scientists used new tests to examine
specimens of the enormous blob. This time they had an answer. The blob was
not the remains of a sea monster, but old blubber from a whale.

1 The best word for the blank in this paragraph is

   Ⓐ remains   Ⓑ expressions   Ⓒ species   Ⓓ skeletons

2 In this paragraph, the word **specimens** must mean

   Ⓐ long claws   Ⓒ tails and fins

   Ⓑ monsters   Ⓓ examples

3 Underline a word or words that helped you answer item 2.

4 Write a sentence of your own using the word **specimens**.

_____

_____

_____

Scholastic Teaching Resources   *Context Clues & Figurative Language*

Context Clues

Read the paragraph. Answer the questions.

Are you good at skipping stones? Some people have the knack, and others are clueless. Researchers did some tests to see what it takes. First, _____ a flat, round stone. When you throw it, add some spin to keep it stable. The heavier the stone, the faster it must be tossed. If it is below a certain **velocity**, the stone will sink. The most important thing is the angle at which the stone hits the water. If it's over 45 degrees, the stone sinks. For the most skips, try for an angle of 20 degrees. That works best.

1 The best word for the blank in this paragraph is

(A) discard   (B) locate   (C) carve   (D) bury

2 In this paragraph, the word **velocity** must mean

(A) sea level   (C) speed

(B) wave height   (D) time of day

3 Underline a word or words that helped you answer item 2.

4 Write a sentence of your own using the word **velocity**.

_____

_____

_____

Name _____   Date _____

Context Clues

Read the paragraph. Answer the questions.

It loves frigid temperatures, snow, and
glacial ice. The polar bear is well _____ to its Arctic
home. This large mammal suffers almost no heat loss in
its North Pole habitat. The polar bear is covered with
a double layer of white fur. Underneath its fur lie four
inches of blubber. The polar bear has large paws that
act as snowshoes and a long snout that it can poke into
ice holes looking for food. This bear is larger than its
ursine cousins, the grizzly and the black bear.

1 The best word for the blank in this paragraph is

(A) dressed   (B) mannered   (C) hardy   (D) suited

2 In this paragraph, the word **ursine** must mean

(A) berry-eating   (C) unbearable

(B) bearlike   (D) barren

3 Underline a word or words that helped you answer item 2.

4 Write a sentence of your own using the word **ursine**.

_____

_____

_____

Scholastic Teaching Resources   *Context Clues & Figurative Language*

Name _____   Date _____

Context Clues

Read the paragraph. Answer the questions.

What's pink and purple and kills? The answer is a
plant called the spotted knapweed. This rather pretty
plant _____ on hillsides, roadsides, rangeland, and
many other parts of the American landscape. But where
the knapweed grows, little else does. That's because the
knapweed releases a poison through its roots into the
soil and kills neighboring plants. The knapweed can
then **appropriate** the water, nutrients, and space that
the other plants would have used.

1 The best word for the blank in this paragraph is

   Ⓐ struggles   Ⓑ interacts   Ⓒ thrives   Ⓓ harvests

2 In this paragraph, the word **appropriate** must mean

   Ⓐ take over   Ⓒ help out

   Ⓑ be correct   Ⓓ appeal to

3 Underline a word or words that helped you answer item 2.

4 Write a sentence of your own using the word **appropriate**.

_____

_____

_____

Context Clues

Read the paragraph. Answer the questions.

A colorful Thanksgiving symbol is the cornucopia. The word *cornucopia* comes from a Latin word that means "horn of plenty." In ancient Rome, a goat's horn was filled with fruit and other foods to _____ Flora, the goddess of flowers, and Fortune, the goddess of fortune or fate. Both in the past and the present, a cornucopia has stood for **abundance**. Thanksgiving is a time when people show their appreciation for a plentiful harvest and other good things in their lives.

1 The best word for the blank in this paragraph is

Ⓐ pester   Ⓑ punish   Ⓒ overflow   Ⓓ represent

2 In this paragraph, the word **abundance** must mean

Ⓐ abandonment   Ⓒ scholarship

Ⓑ great quantity   Ⓓ flower gardens

3 Underline a word or words that helped you answer item 2.

4 Write a sentence of your own using the word **abundance**.

_____

_____

_____

Scholastic Teaching Resources   *Context Clues & Figurative Language*

Context Clues

Read the paragraph. Answer the questions.

Kato is a dog that likes to get around. Kato lives at an amusement park. Many of his hours are spent working as a guard dog on the night _____. But when Kato is off-duty, he likes to ride on the Ferris wheel. In fact, Kato has his own customized car. The benches have been removed so he has enough room, and bowls of food and water are provided. Sometimes Kato rides for hours. Other riders always ask about the Ferris wheel dog, but they aren't allowed to ride in his **compartment**.

1 The best word for the blank in this paragraph is

Ⓐ time   Ⓑ shift   Ⓒ canine   Ⓓ attack

2 In this paragraph, the word **compartment** must mean

Ⓐ a section   Ⓒ workplace

Ⓑ amusement park   Ⓓ curiosity

3 Underline a word or words that helped you answer item 2.

4 Write a sentence of your own using the word **compartment**.

_____

_____

_____

Figurative Language

Read the paragraph. Answer the questions.

The Chinese New Year lasts for 15 days and is observed by Chinese communities the world over. During this time, many special traditions are followed. One is the popular Dragon Dance, when people in a dragon costume twist and prance through the streets. On the last day of the New Year, when the full moon rises, the Chinese celebrate the Lantern Festival. Thousands of <u>paper and silk lanterns twinkle in the dark like magic stars</u>. This happy night embraces the New Year.

1 The underlined words in this paragraph are an example of figurative language called

Ⓐ metaphor   Ⓑ personification   Ⓒ simile   Ⓓ hyperbole

2 These words compare _____ to _____.

3 Find and underline another example of figurative language in the paragraph.

4 This example is called _____.

5 Write the meaning of the second figure of speech in your own words.

_____

_____

Figurative Language

Read the paragraph. Answer the questions.

Do you like a little salt on your food? Many people think <u>food without salt is like eating cardboard</u>. But throughout history, salt has been important not for its flavor but as a way to preserve food. Before there were freezers and refrigerators, meat and fish quickly became rotten. So people soaked or rubbed these foods in salt to keep them from going bad. As a result, salt became as valuable as gold. In fact, soldiers in ancient Rome received part of their wages in salt.

1 The underlined words in this paragraph are an example of figurative language called

   Ⓐ metaphor   Ⓑ personification   Ⓒ simile   Ⓓ hyperbole

2 These words compare _____ to _____.

3 Find and underline another example of figurative language in the paragraph.

4 This example is called _____.

5 Write the meaning of the second figure of speech in your own words.

   _____

   _____

Figurative Language

Read the paragraph. Answer the questions.

For many people, <u>August is a day in the sun</u>. It is a time to go to the beach or the mountains or the woods. With its warm, sunny weather, August invites people to play and relax. Some people also think that August is a good time to smile. These folks belong to the Secret Society of Happy People. On this group's calendar, August is called the National Happiness Happens Month. How do you celebrate this month? Some people do funny things while others just smile a lot. No frowning faces are allowed!

1 The underlined words in this paragraph are an example of figurative language called

   Ⓐ metaphor   Ⓑ personification   Ⓒ simile   Ⓓ hyperbole

2 These words compare _____ to _____.

3 Find and underline another example of figurative language in the paragraph.

4 This example is called _____.

5 Write the meaning of the second figure of speech in your own words.

_____

_____

Scholastic Teaching Resources *Context Clues & Figurative Language*

Figurative Language

Read the paragraph. Answer the questions.

Most flowers are sweet-smelling. In fact, perfumes are made from many flowers. But the rafflesia is <u>such a stinky flower that it makes people regret having a nose</u>! This strange flower grows in the forests of Southeast Asia. Not only is the rafflesia smelly, but one blossom can be as large as a truck tire. Because these flowers are so unusual, many scientists and tourists travel to see them. However, scientists are worried that rafflesias may be in danger of dying out. The forests in which they grow are being cut down.

1 The underlined words in this paragraph are an example of figurative language called

(A) metaphor   (B) personification   (C) simile   (D) hyperbole

2 These words suggest _____.

3 Find and underline another example of figurative language in the paragraph.

4 This example is called _____.

5 Write the meaning of the second figure of speech in your own words.

_____

_____

Scholastic Teaching Resources   Context Clues & Figurative Language

EXERCISE
23

Figurative Language

Read the paragraph. Answer the questions.

<u>The camera spoke for him</u>. In the 1920s and '30s James Van DerZee photographed the people and events in Harlem, a part of New York City. At that time Harlem was home to talented black entertainers, artists, poets, athletes, writers, and politicians. People from all over went to Harlem to enjoy its music, theaters, and nightspots. Van DerZee captured both the famous and the ordinary on film. Many years later, Van DerZee's work was exhibited at an important museum. His photos welcomed people into the past.

1 The underlined words in this paragraph are an example of figurative language called

   (A) metaphor   (B) personification   (C) simile   (D) hyperbole

2 These words suggest _____.

3 Find and underline another example of figurative language in the paragraph.

4 This example is called _____.

5 Write the meaning of the second figure of speech in your own words.

_____

_____

Scholastic Teaching Resources   *Context Clues & Figurative Language*

EXERCISE

24

Figurative Language

Read the paragraph. Answer the questions.

What do you do with your hands on a cool day? You might tuck
them in your pockets. In much the same way, a bird puts its
head under a wing. It does this to keep warm when sleeping.
Birds also are known to stand on one foot while sleeping,
which makes <u>them look like incomplete drawings</u>. There are
two reasons birds do this. They give one leg a rest, and they
keep body heat from escaping through their featherless feet.
You might say that birds are excellent energy conservationists.

1 The underlined words in this paragraph are an example of figurative language called

(A) metaphor   (B) personification   (C) simile   (D) hyperbole

2 These words compare _____ to _____.

3 Find and underline another example of figurative language in the paragraph.

4 This example is called _____.

5 Write the meaning of the second figure of speech in your own words.

_____

_____

Figurative Language

Read the paragraph. Answer the questions.

Have you ever noticed that macadamia nuts are not sold in their shells? If they were, <u>you wouldn't be able to open them in a million years</u>. Their shells are very stubborn. Growers of these nuts say it takes 300 pounds of pressure per square inch to break a macadamia's shell. Before that happens, the nut has to be dried. As it dries, the nut separates from the hard shell. Then a special machine with steel rollers breaks open the shell without damaging the nut.

1 The underlined words in this paragraph are an example of figurative language called

(A) metaphor   (B) personification   (C) simile   (D) hyperbole

2 These words suggest _____.

3 Find and underline another example of figurative language in the paragraph.

4 This example is called _____.

5 Write the meaning of the second figure of speech in your own words.

_____

_____

Scholastic Teaching Resources   Context Clues & Figurative Language

Figurative Language

Read the paragraph. Answer the questions.

The language of William Shakespeare is full of figures of speech. In fact, it is Shakespeare's extraordinary use of language that made him such a great writer. For example, in the play *The Merry Wives of Windsor*, a character says, "Why then, <u>the world's mine oyster</u>." In another play, called *Antony and Cleopatra*, Cleopatra speaks of her love and respect for Antony with these words: "His legs bestrid the ocean; his reared arm crested the world."

1 The underlined words in this paragraph are an example of figurative language called

    Ⓐ metaphor   Ⓑ personification   Ⓒ simile   Ⓓ hyperbole

2 These words compare _____ to _____.

3 Find and underline another example of figurative language in the paragraph.

4 This example is called _____.

5 Write the meaning of the second figure of speech in your own words.

_____

_____

Name _____ Date _____

Figurative Language

Read the paragraph. Answer the questions.

Standing in front of a tornado is as risky as jumping off a cliff.
But scientists have been trying to do something like this so
they can find out how these storms work. In 1981, researchers
designed a container called TOTO (Totable Tornado
Observatory). Inside TOTO were hundreds of pounds of
weather equipment. The idea was to place TOTO in the path of a tornado
so its equipment could pick up information. However, scientists decided the
experiment was as unsafe as a leaky boat and dropped the project.

1 The underlined words in this paragraph are an example of figurative language called

Ⓐ metaphor   Ⓑ personification   Ⓒ simile   Ⓓ hyperbole

2 These words compare _____ to _____.

3 Find and underline another example of figurative language in the paragraph.

4 This example is called _____.

5 Write the meaning of the second figure of speech in your own words.

_____

_____

Scholastic Teaching Resources Context Clues & Figurative Language

Figurative Language

Read the paragraph. Answer the questions.

In 1802, Meriwether Lewis began preparations to explore the land from the Mississippi River to the Rocky Mountains. <u>You would have thought that Lewis was going to the moon.</u> He studied maps. He learned how to take measurements by the stars to figure out directions. He ordered guns and supplies. He talked to geographers, botanists, and zoologists. He had a keelboat built. He chose a coleader, William Clark, and a crew. Adventure called, and in 1804 the team set off.

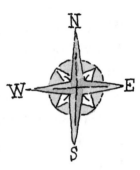

1 The underlined words in this paragraph are an example of figurative language called

Ⓐ metaphor   Ⓑ personification   Ⓒ simile   Ⓓ hyperbole

2 These words suggest _____.

3 Find and underline another example of figurative language in the paragraph.

4 This example is called _____.

5 Write the meaning of the second figure of speech in your own words.

_____

_____

Figurative Language

Read the paragraph. Answer the questions.

<u>A shoe by the roadside is an untold story.</u>
Where is the mate? How did it get there?
Many people are curious about shoes lying
on the sides of roads. They have come up
with several explanations. One idea is that the shoes
were tossed out of cars by children during arguments. Another idea is that hikers
accidentally dropped a shoe. A third theory is that the shoes fell out of garbage
trucks. No one knows for sure. These single roadside shoes don't tell their secret.

1 The underlined words in this paragraph are an example of figurative language called

Ⓐ metaphor   Ⓑ personification   Ⓒ simile   Ⓓ hyperbole

2 These words compare _____ to _____.

3 Find and underline another example of figurative language in the paragraph.

4 This example is called _____.

5 Write the meaning of the second figure of speech in your own words.

_____

_____

Figurative Language

Read the paragraph. Answer the questions.

<u>You don't know winter if you haven't tried snowboarding</u>.
This winter sport began about 50 years ago in Vermont.
To many fans, snowboarding is a ride on a frozen wave.
It is a combination of surfing and skiing that takes thrill
seekers down snow-covered mountains. Many boarders
also perform stunts such as soaring into the air in a
maneuver called a half-pipe. Snowboarding became an
Olympic sport in the 1998 Winter Games in Nagano, Japan.

1 The underlined words in this paragraph are an example of figurative language called

   Ⓐ metaphor   Ⓑ personification   Ⓒ simile   Ⓓ hyperbole

2 These words suggest _____.

3 Find and underline another example of figurative language in the paragraph.

4 This example is called _____.

5 Write the meaning of the second figure of speech in your own words.

_____

_____

Figurative Language

Read the paragraph. Answer the questions.

<u>Do words buy votes</u>? Many candidates for public office think so. Certain words are used over and over again in their speeches. For example, the word *hope* in a candidate's speech is as predictable as the sunrise. Another likely word is *jobs*. Most candidates also throw in words such as *values* and *strength*. When candidates are running for national office, they almost always bring up the words *health care* and *economy*. Candidates use these words to tap into the concerns of voters.

1 The underlined words in this paragraph are an example of figurative language called

(A) metaphor   (B) personification   (C) simile   (D) hyperbole

2 These words suggest _____.

3 Find and underline another example of figurative language in the paragraph.

4 This example is called _____.

5 Write the meaning of the second figure of speech in your own words.

_____

_____

Figurative Language

Read the paragraph. Answer the questions.

<u>Animal tails tell many tales</u>. In most cases, an animal's tail serves a helpful function. For example, the tail of a bird helps it fly. A porcupine's tail is a weapon. The porcupine uses the many quills in its tail to defend itself. A horse uses its tail to keep away flies. Fish, of course, use their tails to help them swim. What does an elephant use its tail for? A baby elephant holds onto its mother's tail with its trunk so it doesn't get lost. Kangaroos use their tails for balance. They can also sit on their tails!

1 The underlined words in this paragraph are an example of figurative language called

Ⓐ metaphor   Ⓑ personification   Ⓒ simile   Ⓓ hyperbole

2 These words suggest _____.

3 Find and underline another example of figurative language in the paragraph.

4 This example is called _____.

5 Write the meaning of the second figure of speech in your own words.

_____

_____

Figurative Language

Read the paragraph. Answer the questions.

<u>The luge is the most thrilling sport in the universe.</u> This high-speed event has been part of the Winter Olympics since 1964. Athletes compete on small sleds usually made of fiberglass. They lie on their backs with their feet stretched out over the front of the sled and race down a curved, ice-covered course. To steer, the rider must use leg and foot pressure on the sled's runners and downward pressure with his or her shoulders. A rider's moves must be as exacting as a surgeon's knife.

1 The underlined words in this paragraph are an example of figurative language called

Ⓐ metaphor   Ⓑ personification   Ⓒ simile   Ⓓ hyperbole

2 These words suggest _____.

3 Find and underline another example of figurative language in the paragraph.

4 This example is called _____.

5 Write the meaning of the second figure of speech in your own words.

_____

_____

Scholastic Teaching Resources   Context Clues & Figurative Language

Figurative Language

Read the paragraph. Answer the questions.

Each fall, monarch butterflies migrate from northern regions to warmer areas further south. These butterflies always go to the same place. Often they rest in the same trees, <u>painting the green branches a vivid orange</u>. A monarch can fly up to 12 miles an hour and cover almost 100 miles a day. Sometimes more than 1,000 monarchs travel together. The migrating butterflies head for Florida, Southern California, and Mexico. There, they enjoy warm winter vacations.

1 The underlined words in this paragraph are an example of figurative language called

(A) metaphor   (B) personification   (C) simile   (D) hyperbole

2 These words suggest _____.

3 Find and underline another example of figurative language in the paragraph.

4 This example is called _____.

5 Write the meaning of the second figure of speech in your own words.

_____

_____

Figurative Language

Read the paragraph. Answer the questions.

<u>Sometimes laws can seem as silly as a clown's clothes.</u> Usually, these are laws that were once made for a reason but are no longer needed. Here are some funny laws from Canada. In Saskatoon, you cannot catch fish with your hands. In Calgary, it's against the law to toss snowballs without the mayor's permission. Children can't eat ice cream cones on the streets of Ottawa on Sundays. Places in the U.S. have strange laws, too. Some make as much sense as a talking turtle.

1 The underlined words in this paragraph are an example of figurative language called

Ⓐ metaphor   Ⓑ personification   Ⓒ simile   Ⓓ hyperbole

2 These words compare _____ to _____.

3 Find and underline another example of figurative language in the paragraph.

4 This example is called _____.

5 Write the meaning of the second figure of speech in your own words.

_____

_____

Scholastic Teaching Resources   Context Clues & Figurative Language

Context Clues

Read the paragraph. Answer the questions.

When you're driving on a highway, you often see huge advertisements posted along the roadside. Many people think these _____ are unattractive, and they have been banned in some communities. City planners call them "litter on a stick." This term is one of many that planners have developed to describe humanmade features of the landscape. Many of these terms are related to the **sprawl** of communities as they grow without any real planning.

1 A possible word for the blank in this paragraph is _____.

2 I chose this word because _____.

3 A possible meaning for the word **sprawl** in the paragraph might be

_____.

4 I think so because _____

_____.

Figurative Language

Read the paragraph. Answer the questions.

Geckos are known for their ability to climb on any surface and never lose their grip. Now scientists have discovered that geckos' feet are self-cleaning. A gecko can step through all kinds of dirt, but its feet stay as clean as a whistle. That's because there are millions of tiny hairs on a gecko's foot. These help to counteract the force of gravity and to repel dirt. Scientists hope to use the gecko's foot as a model for products that help people, such as bandages that don't leave a sticky mark when they are removed.

1 Write a figure of speech from the paragraph. _____

_____

2 This figure of speech is called a _____.

3 The figure of speech in the paragraph means _____

_____.

Name _____   Date _____

Student Record

Date	Exercise #	Number Correct	Comments

Scholastic Teaching Resources   *Context Clues & Figurative Language*

Answers

page 8:
1. B; communal, medieval; delight
2. D
3. Possible: outdoor area within the walls

page 9:
1. D
2. Answers will vary.

page 10:
1. C   2. D
3. Possible: alone; solitary
4. Answers will vary.

page 11:
1. A   2. C
3. Possible: stay in the museum
4. Answers will vary.

page 12:
1. D   2. B
3. Possible: rot; fresh reeds
4. Answers will vary.

page 13:
1. B   2. A
3. Possible: green algae; green treetops; escape
4. Answers will vary.

page 14:
1. C   2. B
3. Possible: violent; rage; wash away
4. Answers will vary.

page 15:
1. D   2. A
3. Possible: instead of; it steals; sucks up nutrients
4. Answers will vary.

page 16:
1. B   2. B
3. Possible: stripped away
4. Answers will vary.

page 17:
1. A   2. C
3. Possible: marked their choices; paper
4. Answers will vary.

page 18:
1. C   2. D
3. Possible: everyday use by ordinary people; design is traditional to the group that builds them
4. Answers will vary.

page 19:
1. C   2. B
3. Possible: play as they wished
4. Answers will vary.

page 20:
1. D   2. A

3. Possible: holds out his arms; "Come on! Everyone needs a hug"
4. Answers will vary.

page 21:
1. B   2. D
3. Possible: popular
4. Answers will vary.

page 22:
1. A   2. D
3. Possible: tests; examine
4. Answers will vary.

page 23:
1. B   2. C
3. Possible: the faster it must be tossed
4. Answers will vary.

page 24:
1. D   2. B
3. Possible: grizzly; black bear
4. Answers will vary.

page 25:
1. C   2. A
3. Possible: that the other plants would have used
4. Answers will vary.

page 26:
1. D   2. B
3. Possible: horn of plenty; plentiful harvest
4. Answers will vary.

page 27:
1. B   2. A
3. Possible: car
4. Answers will vary.

page 28:
1. C
2. lanterns to magic stars
3. This happy night embraces the New Year.
4. personification
5. Answers will vary.

page 29:
1. C
2. food without salt to eating cardboard
3. Salt became as valuable as gold.
4. simile
5. Answers will vary.

page 30:
1. A
2. August to a day in the sun
3. August invites people to play and relax.
4. personification
5. Answers will vary.

page 31:
1. D
2. the smell of a rafflesia is extremely bad

3. One blossom can be as large as a truck tire.
4. simile
5. Answers will vary.

page 32:
1. B
2. the camera expressed his thoughts
3. His photos welcomed people into the past.
4. personification
5. Answers will vary.

page 33:
1. C
2. birds on one foot to incomplete drawings
3. Birds are excellent energy conservationists.
4. metaphor
5. Answers will vary.

page 34:
1. D
2. it's very difficult to crack open a macadamia shell
3. Their shells are very stubborn.
4. personification
5. Answers will vary.

page 35:
1. A
2. the world to an oyster
3. His legs bestrid the ocean; his reared arm crested the world.
4. hyperbole
5. Answers will vary.

page 36:
1. C
2. standing in front of a tornado to jumping off a cliff
3. The experiment was as unsafe as a leaky boat.
4. simile
5. Answers will vary.

page 37:
1. D
2. how carefully Lewis planned
3. Adventure called.
4. personification
5. Answers will vary.

page 38:
1. A
2. a shoe by the roadside to an untold story
3. Roadside shoes don't tell their secret.
4. personification
5. Answers will vary.

page 39:
1. D

2. the excitement of snowboarding
3. Snowboarding is a ride on a frozen wave.
4. metaphor
5. Answers will vary.

page 40:
1. B
2. words are so powerful they take on human qualities
3. The word *hope* in a candidate's speech is as predictable as the sunrise.
4. simile
5. Answers will vary.

page 41:
1. B
2. animals' tails contain a lot of information
3. A porcupine's tail is a weapon.
4. metaphor
5. Answers will vary.

page 42:
1. D
2. nothing is as exciting as the luge
3. A rider's moves must be as exacting as a surgeon's knife.
4. simile
5. Answers will vary.

page 43:
1. B
2. how monarchs look in a tree
3. They enjoy warm winter vacations.
4. personification
5. Answers will vary.

page 44:
1. C
2. laws to a clown's clothes
3. Some [laws] make as much sense as a talking turtle.
4. simile
5. Answers will vary.

page 45:
1. Possible: billboards; signs
2. Possible: a huge advertisement along the road could be a billboard
3. Possible: unchecked or haphazard growth
4. Possible: communities grow without planning

page 46:
1. Its feet stay as clean as a whistle.
2. simile
3. a gecko's feet don't get dirty

Scholastic Teaching Resources   Context Clues & Figurative Language